LONDON, NEW YORK, MELBOURNE,
MUNICH, AND DELHI

Written by John Woodward
Illustrations by Gary Hanna

Senior editor Shaila Brown
Senior art editor Vicky Short
Designer Richard Horsford
Jacket designer Mark Cavanagh

Production editor Ben Marcus
Production controller Erika Pepe
Managing editor Julie Ferris
Managing art editor Owen Peyton Jones
Publisher Sarah Larter
Associate publishing director Liz Wheeler
Art director Phil Ormerod
Publishing director Jonathan Metcalf

Consultant Dr. Kim Bryan

First published in the United States
in 2012 by DK Publishing
375 Hudson Street, New York, New York 10014

A catalog record for this book
is available from the Library of Congress.

ISBN 978-0-7566-9237-7

Printed and bound in China by Hung Hing

Discover more at
www.dk.com

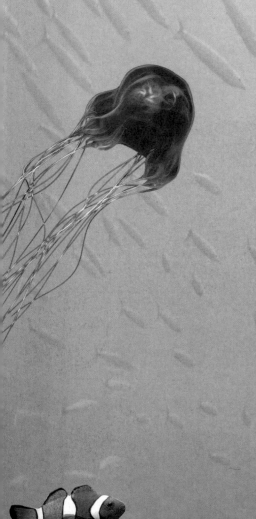

LOOK CLOSER
OCEAN

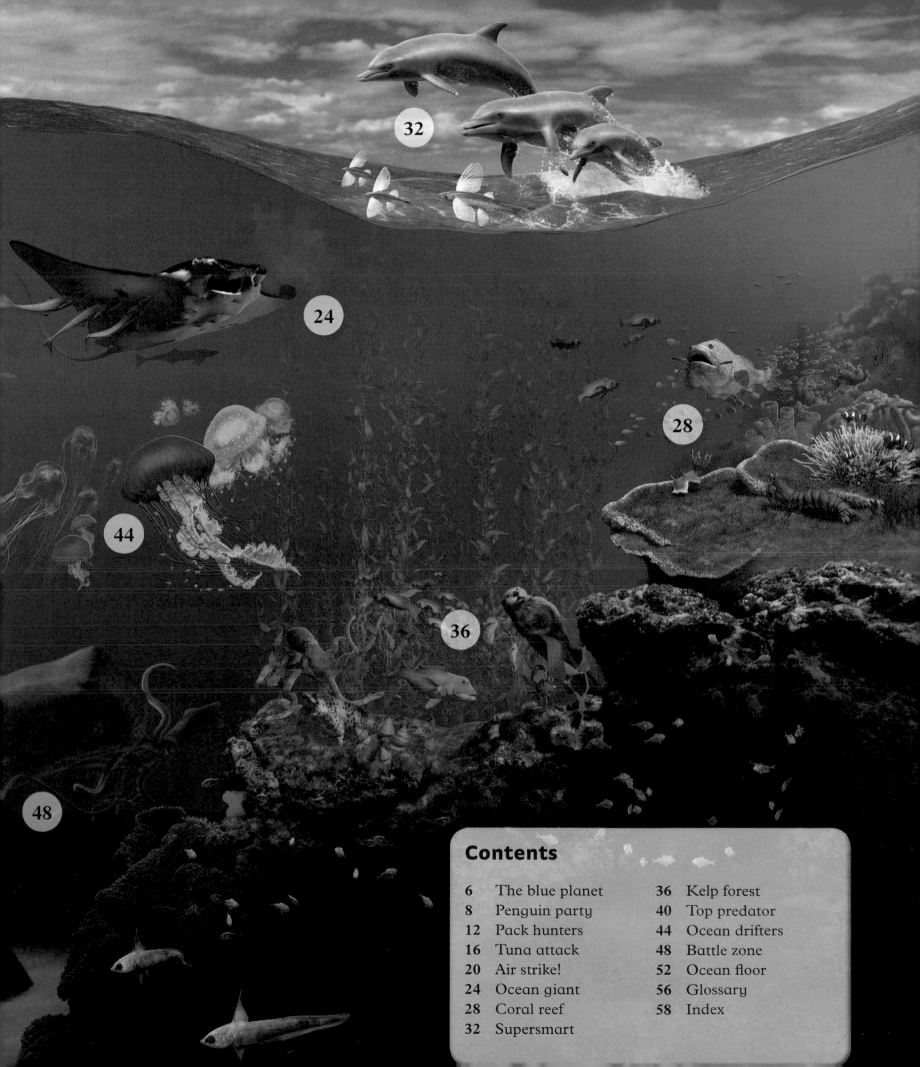

Contents

The blue planet

Deep oceans cover more than two-thirds of Earth's surface, making our planet look blue from space. The oceans form the world's biggest habitat for life, from the icy fringes of the frozen poles to the warm and magical coral seas of the tropics. Living in these oceans are the largest and most spectacular creatures on Earth, as well as some of the planet's deadliest killers.

Life on Earth probably began in the oceans, more than 3.5 billion years ago.

The world's oceans

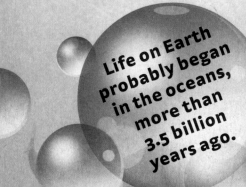

ARCTIC OCEAN

All the world's oceans are joined together, forming a single global ocean. The five main parts of the global ocean have their own names. The biggest part is the Pacific Ocean, which covers a third of the globe. The Atlantic Ocean is the second largest, followed by the Indian Ocean. The Southern Ocean surrounds Antarctica and is the world's stormiest ocean. At the north pole is the Arctic Ocean, which freezes over every winter.

Pacific

If visitors from space came to Earth and arrived over the Pacific Ocean, they might think that water covers the whole world. The Pacific is larger than all Earth's land area combined and includes the deepest point in all the oceans. Its name means peaceful, though it's sometimes battered by violent tropical storms.

Ocean depth zones

The Sun's warmth and light makes the surface of the ocean warm and sunny, but the water gets colder and darker as you travel deeper. Eventually the light fades out altogether, so the deep ocean is a place of permanent, near-freezing darkness.

Sunlit zone
Life flourishes in the warm, sunlit surface waters of the sea. At least 80 percent of marine animals live within 660 ft (200 m) of the surface.

Twilight zone
Below the sunlit zone lies a world of cold blue twilight, where deep divers such as the sperm whale hunt the strange creatures of the deep.

Dark zone
Below 3,300 ft (1,000 m) there is no sunlight at all, only the eerie glow of weird, luminous animals flashing light signals to each other in the dark.

There are more than 20,000 islands in the Pacific, nearly all surrounded by coral reefs.

A penguin has to catch one krill every six seconds to feed its chicks.

Flightless divers

1 Adélie penguin
2 Torpedo-shaped body
3 Dense, waterproof feathers
4 Strong flipperlike wings
5 Sharp bill
6 Shrimplike krill

Penguin party

Adélie penguins spend most of their lives on the floating sea ice that surrounds Antarctica, diving into the cold ocean to prey on swarming krill. Like all penguins they are graceful swimmers and divers, but clumsy on their feet. Penguins cannot fly. Their wings act as flippers, driving them through the water. Each spring Adélie penguins return to land to lay their eggs and rear their chicks, but they soon move back out to sea.

Ready...

Icebergs and floating pack ice make welcome landing sites for Adélie penguins between fishing expeditions. Here they are usually safe from enemies such as killer whales and leopard seals. Sooner or later the penguins must take the plunge and dive in search of their main prey—krill.

Adélie penguins don't hunt when they are nesting and can go hungry for up to 35 days.

Set...

Penguins can look comical on land as they waddle around on their short legs, or even toboggan over ice and snow on their bellies. But when they dive into the water they are transformed into elegant sea creatures. Of all ocean birds, penguins are the best suited to underwater life. Their wings work as flippers, three layers of short feathers keep out the cold, and heavy bones make deep diving easier.

Antarctic neighbors

Emperor penguins

The biggest penguins, emperors breed on sea ice, where the males keep their eggs warm by resting them on their feet. They do this for 60 days, through the worst of the Antarctic winter. When the chicks are born the penguin parents feed them until they can hunt for themselves.

Leopard seal

Unlike other seals, the leopard seal is a powerful predator. It targets small penguins such as Adélies, lurking near the edge of the ice to ambush them as they dive into the water.

Poles apart

Polar bear
In the far north, the Arctic Ocean pack ice is the hunting ground of the mighty polar bear. It preys mainly on seals, waiting by holes in the floating ice to seize them as they come up for air. If there is no ice it cannot hunt, so warmer summers threaten its survival.

Walrus
Big herds of walruses gather on remote Arctic shores and floating pack ice. Their spectacular tusks are status symbols, like a stag's antlers, but both male and female walruses have them. They eat shellfish, feeling for them on the seabed with their sensitive whiskers.

There are no twigs in Antarctica so Adélie penguins make their nests out of stones instead.

A special blood circulation system keeps penguins from losing vital body heat through their feet, but this means their feet are always cold.

Go...

Hunting penguins "fly" through the water, using their tails and feet to steer. Although not particularly fast, they are very agile, which helps them target their prey. Adélie penguins can dive 560 ft (170 m) below the surface, but they rarely need to swim so deep to find a meal.

The prey

Antarctic krill are shrimplike animals that live in the open ocean. They feed on microscopic floating algae, and when these are abundant in summer the krill multiply to form vast swarms that can tint the ocean red.

Pack hunters

Hungry killer whales patrol the oceans in small groups looking for prey. They may attack anything from shoals of fish to giant blue whales, but they usually target dolphins, penguins, sea lions, and seals. They work together to ambush or encircle their victims, even tipping or smashing floating ice to topple seals into the water and into their gaping jaws.

The remains of 30 seals were once found in the stomach of a killer whale.

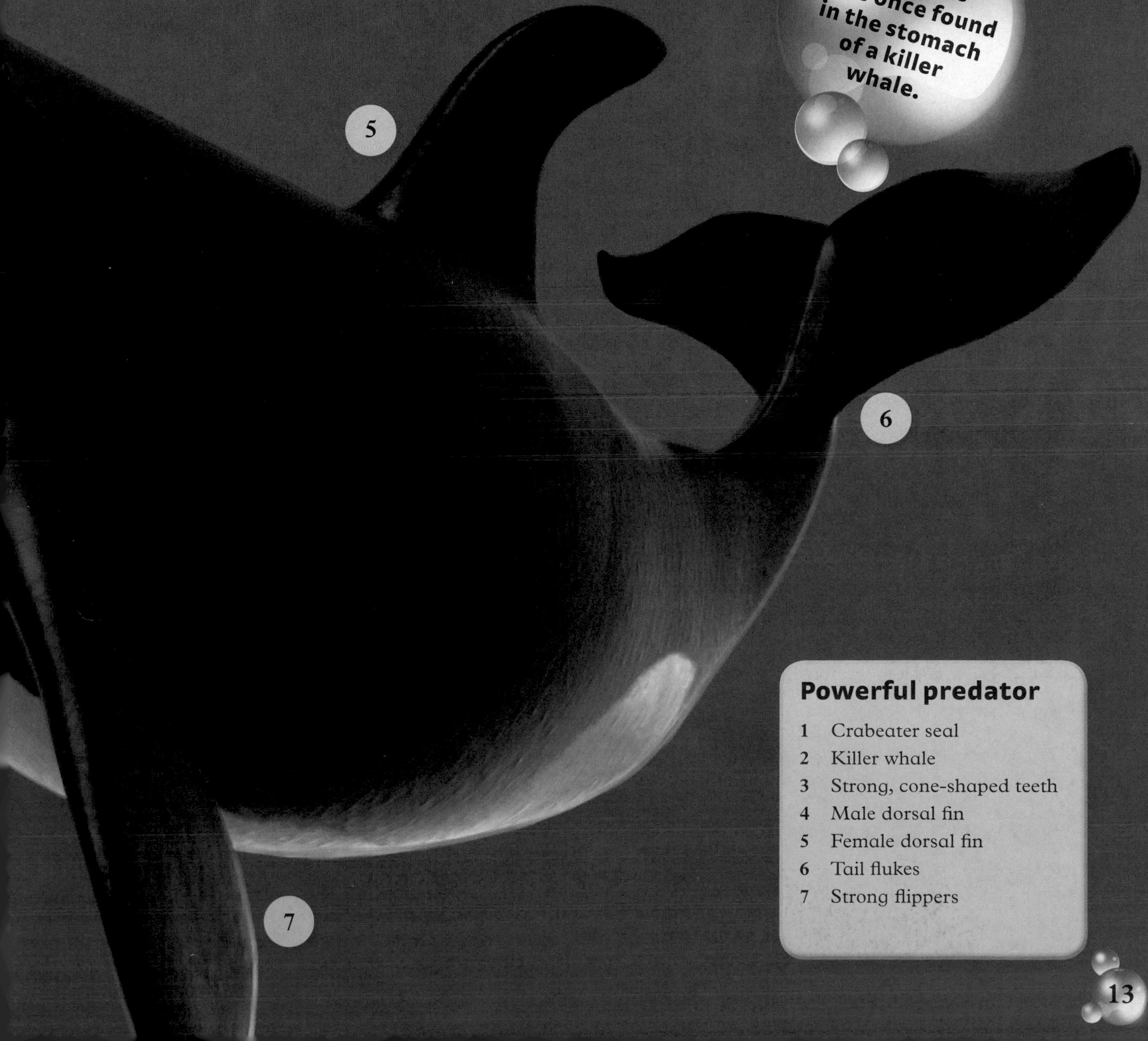

5

6

7

Powerful predator

1 Crabeater seal
2 Killer whale
3 Strong, cone-shaped teeth
4 Male dorsal fin
5 Female dorsal fin
6 Tail flukes
7 Strong flippers

Speedy retreat

This crabeater seal will need to move fast
to escape the fearsome jaws of the killer
whale. Millions of crabeaters live in the
cold Southern Ocean around Antarctica,
where they use their specialized sievelike
teeth to feed on swarming krill.

Pod life

The long dorsal fin of this killer whale shows that
it is a male, traveling with a group of females.
These groups are called pods. They are families
led by an older female—probably the male's
mother. The other females are likely to be his
sisters. They may stay together for life, but
they mate with whales from other pods.

A killer whale
is big enough
to swallow a
seal whole in
a single gulp.

Wonderful whales

Pilot whale

Pilot whales are very sociable animals. They live in big herds of up to 100, and sometimes more, feeding mainly on squid in cool seas to the north and south of the tropics. They prefer open oceans, but sometimes a whole herd ends up mysteriously stranded on a beach.

Beluga

Adult belugas are pure white, unlike any other whale. They live in the far north near the Arctic ice, traveling in groups that usually swim near the ocean surface preying on fish. They often move from one area of open water to another by following narrow channels through the floating pack ice.

Narwhal

Another Arctic whale that lives near the sea ice, the narwhal is famous for its single spiral tusk, which can be up to 10 ft (3 m) long. Only males have tusks, which they use for showing off to rivals—although sometimes they fight with them. These tusks were once very valuable because people thought they came from unicorns!

Whale attack

No matter how fast the crabeater seal swims, it stands little chance of evading the hunting killer whales. These animals are big, powerful, and extremely intelligent. If the seal manages to avoid this attack and climb onto the sea ice, they will find another way to catch it. Groups of killer whales may swim in formation beneath an ice floe to create a wave that washes over it, sweeping a resting seal into the sea. Once it is seized by a killer whale's big pointed teeth, it has no hope of escape.

Tuna attack

Swarms of tiny animals drifting in the ocean as plankton feed glittering shoals of herring and other small fish. The silvery shoals attract hunters such as these tuna. The tuna attack at high speeds, scaring the smaller fish into a tight, swirling bait ball as each tries to hide behind the others. The tuna simply charge in and snatch as many fish as they want.

Some tuna can accelerate to a shattering top speed of 50 mph (80 kph).

1

2

3

Efficient hunters

1   Bluefin tuna
2   Long pectoral fins
3   Crescent-shaped tail
4   Robust body
5   Herring bait ball

High-speed hunters

Sailfish

The fastest fish of all, the sailfish can rocket through the ocean at 62 mph (100 kph). Its sharp bill helps its streamlined body pierce the water, and a superefficient breathing system ensures that it never runs out of oxygen.

Shortfin mako shark

The mako shark is a close relative of the fearsome great white shark, but this shark is mainly a fish eater. When attacking speedy prey such as tuna, it can knife through the water at up to 45 mph (72 kph).

Barracuda

Notorious for its mouthful of sharp, fanglike teeth, the great barracuda relies on speed to catch its prey by surprise. It attacks anything that glints in the water, and often trails sharks to scavenge leftover scraps.

Safety in numbers

Small fish such as these herring often swim in shoals. This is safer for them, since only the fish on the outside of the shoal are exposed to enemies. During an attack, they bunch up into a dense ball, but this doesn't always save them, especially if there are a lot of hunters.

Built for speed

Tuna can swim with amazing speed. Large, powerful muscles transmit power to the crescent-shaped tail so effectively that a tuna can outaccelerate a high-powered sports car. The fins fold into slots to improve streamlining when the fish is moving fast.

Some herring shoals contain millions of fish swimming in formation.

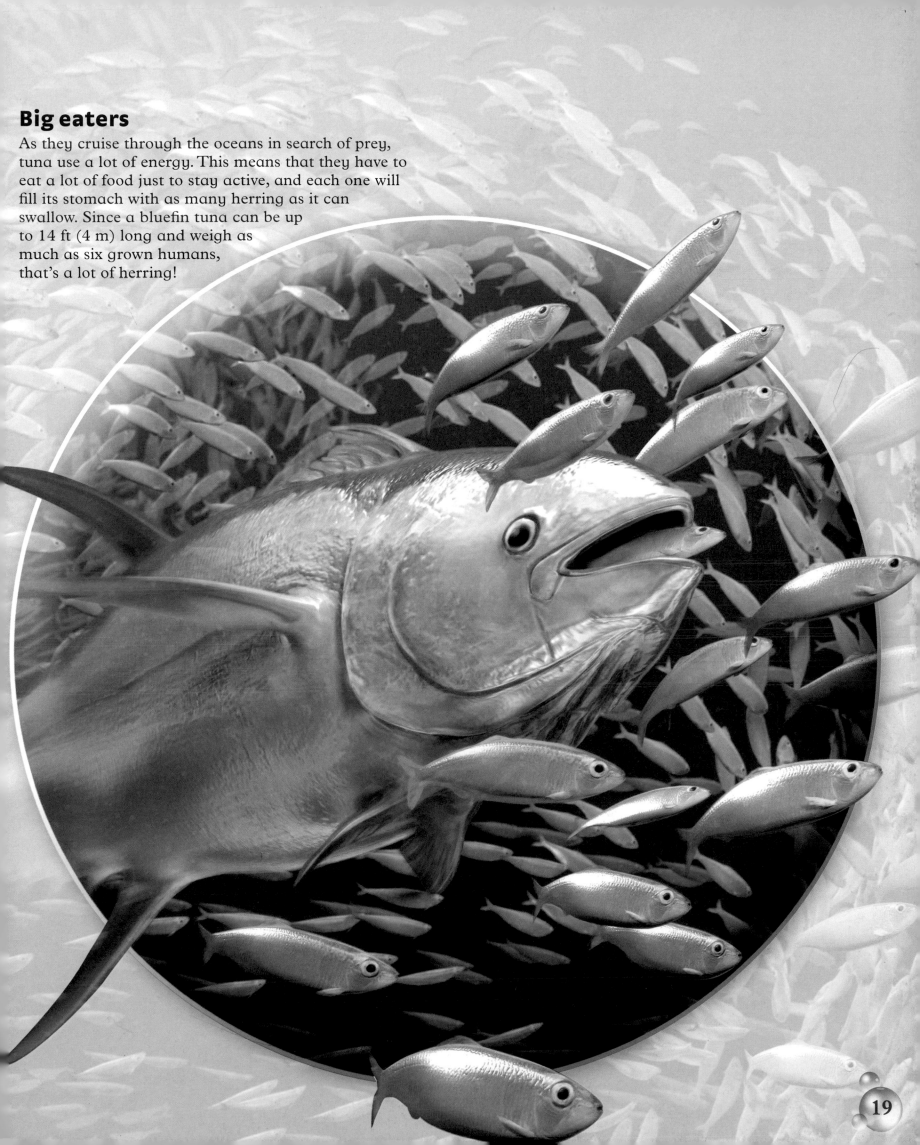

Big eaters

As they cruise through the oceans in search of prey, tuna use a lot of energy. This means that they have to eat a lot of food just to stay active, and each one will fill its stomach with as many herring as it can swallow. Since a bluefin tuna can be up to 14 ft (4 m) long and weigh as much as six grown humans, that's a lot of herring!

Air strike!

When shoals of fish are attacked from below and try to escape, they are driven toward the surface. The commotion attracts ocean birds such as these gannets, which use a spectacular diving technique to join the feeding frenzy. Plunging from the sky with their wings swept back like arrowheads, they slice into the water at incredible speeds. They chase after the fish underwater, seizing them in their long bills and swallowing them headfirst.

3

A gannet can plunge 20 ft (6 m) below the waves if it dives from high enough.

4

5

Plunge-divers

1 Diving gannet
2 Long, sweeping wings
3 Sharp-edged bill
4 Broad webbed feet
5 Herring shoal

Flying underwater

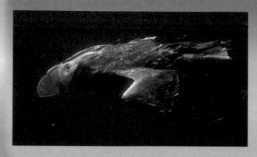

Puffin
Most diving seabirds use their webbed feet for underwater swimming. But some, like this tufted puffin, use their wings instead. The wings have to be shorter than usual to work underwater, which makes true flying hard work.

Headfirst

Gannets swallow a lot of fish while they are still underwater, but sometimes a gannet brings a fish to the surface. It shakes it vigorously, juggles it in its bill, then swallows it headfirst so its spiny fin rays and scales don't stick in its throat.

Big mouthful

The gannet's long daggerlike bill has sharp saw-toothed edges for gripping slippery, struggling fish such as herring, mackerel, and even cod and small salmon. Since it cannot rip its victims apart, it has to swallow them whole, and this limits the size of fish it can swallow. Even so, its elastic throat allows it to gulp down flatfish the size of a small plate.

Breeding gannets gather in huge island colonies of up to 60,000 pairs.

High velocity

As it hurtles down in a near-vertical dive, a gannet rakes its wings farther and farther back until their tips are almost touching each other, so it plunges into the sea at maximum speed. Its streamlined bill and head pierce the water like a spear, but despite this it often makes a big splash. Small air pockets under the skin of its face and chest help cushion the shock of impact.

Out of the blue

Plunging into the shoal as if from nowhere, the gannet takes the fish by surprise and often manages to seize one while it is still knifing down through the water. If it misses, the gannet doubles back through the shoal and tries to grab a fish on the way up to the surface, chasing after it if necessary.

All at sea

Arctic terns
Many ocean birds travel vast distances. Arctic terns breed in the far north, but as winter approaches they fly halfway around the world to feed among the Antarctic pack ice, returning to the Arctic to breed again in the spring.

Albatross
The wandering albatross spends most of its life at sea, soaring over the waves of the stormy Southern Ocean. It rides the winds like a glider, holding its amazingly long, slender wings rigidly outspread.

Kittiwakes
Ocean birds cannot lay their eggs at sea, so they return to nest on the fringes of the land. Many, like these kittiwakes, form big, noisy cliff colonies, while other ocean birds, such as puffins, nest in burrows.

Ocean giant

The biggest fish in the oceans are the giant filter-feeding sharks and rays. The spectacular manta ray feeds by swimming slowly through clouds of plankton with its mouth open, straining the water through its sievelike gills to catch tiny drifting animals. It makes long journeys across tropical oceans in search of plankton-rich feeding areas, often in the company of remora fish that cling to its underside.

A manta can grow to a colossal 25 ft (7.5 m) from tip to tip of its broad "wings."

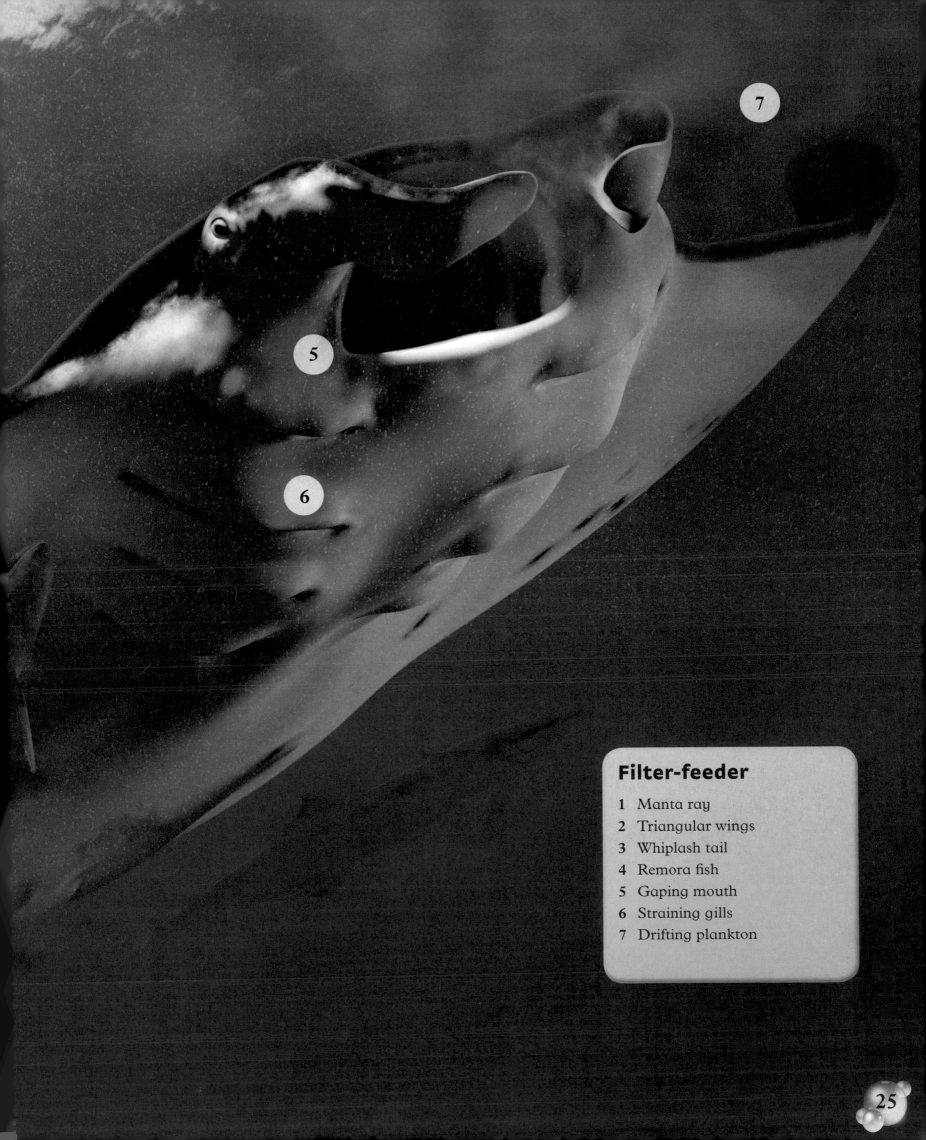

Filter-feeder

1 Manta ray
2 Triangular wings
3 Whiplash tail
4 Remora fish
5 Gaping mouth
6 Straining gills
7 Drifting plankton

Giant filter-feeders

Blue whale
Up to 100 ft (30 m) long, the blue whale is the largest animal on Earth. It feeds by taking a huge gulp of water, forcing it out through a mesh of prey-trapping fibers lining its mouth.

Whale shark
By far the largest fish in the sea, growing to 39 ft (12 m), this tropical giant feeds like a manta, by straining water through its gills. It scoops up tiny plankton as it swims close to the water's surface.

Basking shark
The harmless basking shark travels huge distances to find food in plankton-rich cooler oceans. It cruises along with its mouth gaping open, filtering the water to gather prey.

Hitchhikers

Sometimes called suckerfish, remoras travel through the oceans by attaching themselves to bigger fish such as manta rays. Each remora has an oval sucker on top of its head that grips the manta's smooth skin, but the remora can let go at any time to gather up scraps of food.

Jumbo wings

By slowly beating its long triangular wings, the graceful manta seems to fly effortlessly through the water. It sometimes leaps into the air, falling back with a dramatic splash.

Dragnet

Although the manta does have tiny teeth, it never uses them. It just opens its mouth wide as it swims forward, and uses the flexible lobes on each side of its head to funnel water and tiny drifting animals into its mouth. As the water flows through its mouth cavity and out through the gill slits below, the manta strains off the animals and swallows them.

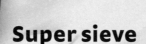

Super sieve

Like all fish, the manta has feathery blood-filled gills that absorb vital oxygen from the water flowing through its mouth. The delicate gills are protected by grids called gill rakers that act like sieves, straining the water to catch small animals. These pass to the back of the mouth where the manta can swallow them.

Mantas usually travel alone, but sometimes hundreds gather in one place to feed.

Filtered food

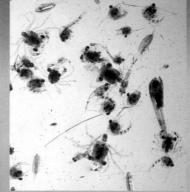

Plankton prey

Most of the manta's prey are extremely small creatures that drift in the water as plankton. They include shrimplike copepods, baby crabs, miniature prawns, newly hatched fish, and the free-floating young of clams and barnacles.

Coral reef

Teeming with life and full of dazzling colors, coral reefs look like underwater gardens. These tropical wonders are created not by plants but by tiny animals called corals, which look like flowers and grow by the millions on the seafloor. Corals have hard, stony skeletons that stay in place when they die, building up to make the reef grow.

Corals live in huge colonies, joined together like the twigs of a tree.

Life on the reef

1 Giant grouper
2 Bluestreak cleaner fish
3 Green puller fish
4 Sea slug
5 Table coral
6 Fairy basslet fish
7 Fan coral
8 Weedy scorpionfish
9 Brain coral
10 Tube sponge
11 Clownfish
12 Blue starfish
13 Sea anemone
14 Peacock mantis shrimp

Scientists estimate that some coral reefs began growing more than 50 million years ago.

Cleaning up

This giant grouper is having its teeth cleaned! The small blue fish around its mouth are bluestreak cleaner wrasses, which live by picking bits of food and bloodsucking parasites off the teeth, skin, and gills of bigger fish. This helps keep the big fish healthy, and they know it, so they are very happy to let the cleaners get on with their work.

Underwater garden

Brain coral
Like most reef corals, a brain coral is a colony of hundreds of tiny animals, all joined together. The whole colony is supported by a stony skeleton, forming a rocky dome that looks like a brain.

Sea fan
A sea fan is a coral that does not have a stony skeleton. The tiny animals of the colony live on tough, flexible branches that look like those of a plant, and sift food from the water that flows past them.

Table coral
The golden color of this table coral comes from microscopic algae that live inside the bodies of the coral animals. The algae capture the energy in sunlight and use it to make food, which the corals absorb.

Tube sponges
Dotted among the corals are sponges—colonies of simple animals supported by spongy skeletons. They draw water through tiny pores in the tube walls, strain it for food particles, and pump it out the top.

Reef dazzlers

Coral reefs are alive with vividly colored fish, such as these green pullers and orange fairy basslets. The different colors help the fish know who's who, and some may even act as camouflage.

Pretty in pink

On a coral reef, even the slugs are beautiful. These sea slugs glide over the coral, grazing on small seaweeds and attached animals. Their tentacles often contain stinging cells taken from their prey. These do not harm the sea slugs and are used to defend them from their enemies.

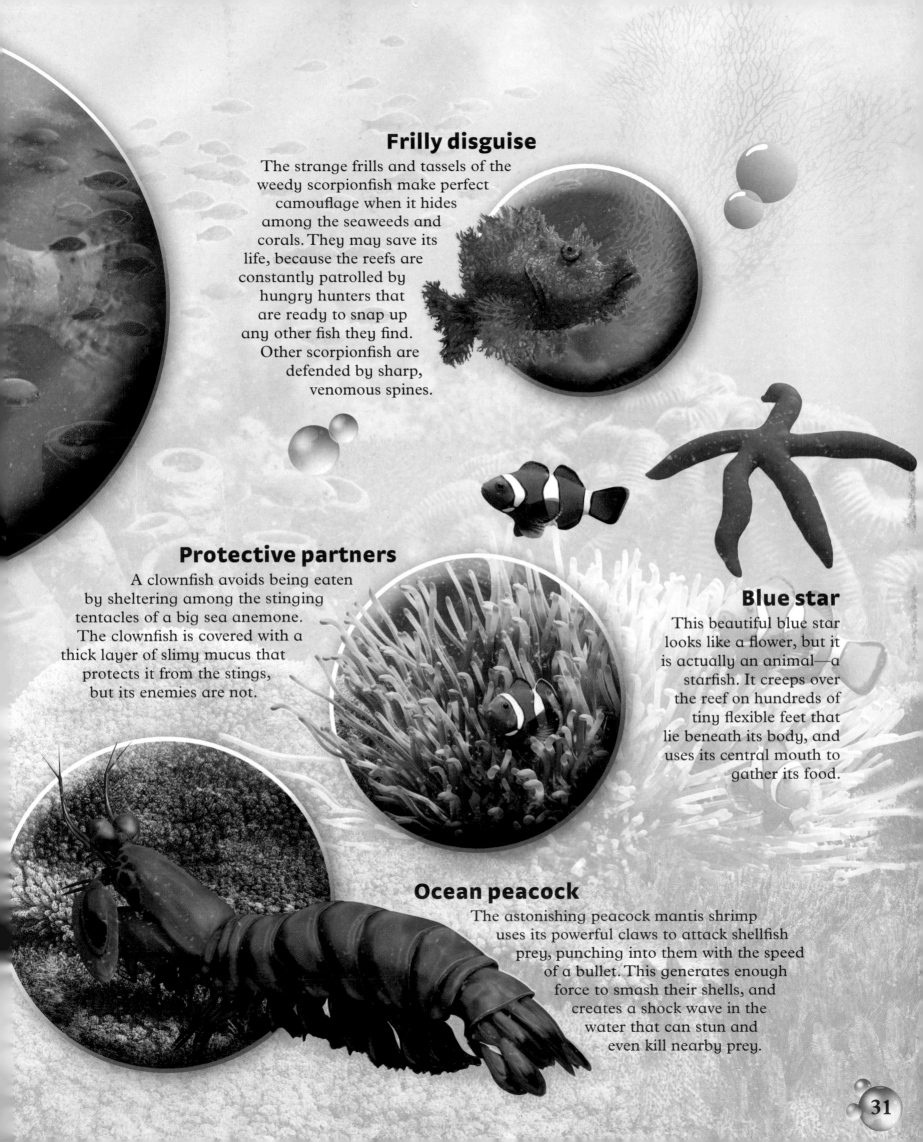

Frilly disguise

The strange frills and tassels of the weedy scorpionfish make perfect camouflage when it hides among the seaweeds and corals. They may save its life, because the reefs are constantly patrolled by hungry hunters that are ready to snap up any other fish they find. Other scorpionfish are defended by sharp, venomous spines.

Protective partners

A clownfish avoids being eaten by sheltering among the stinging tentacles of a big sea anemone. The clownfish is covered with a thick layer of slimy mucus that protects it from the stings, but its enemies are not.

Blue star

This beautiful blue star looks like a flower, but it is actually an animal—a starfish. It creeps over the reef on hundreds of tiny flexible feet that lie beneath its body, and uses its central mouth to gather its food.

Ocean peacock

The astonishing peacock mantis shrimp uses its powerful claws to attack shellfish prey, punching into them with the speed of a bullet. This generates enough force to smash their shells, and creates a shock wave in the water that can stun and even kill nearby prey.

Supersmart

Fast, agile, and highly intelligent, bottlenose dolphins are dazzlingly efficient hunters of fish and squid. They are small, toothed whales, so highly specialized for life at sea that they can outswim most fish. They travel across oceans in groups called pods that stay in touch using a variety of sounds. They also use the echoes of sound pulses to target prey in cloudy water or darkness, and work together to outsmart it.

Ocean racers

1   Bottlenose dolphin
2   Curved flippers
3   Sharp, conical teeth
4   Powerful tail
5   Flying fish

Dolphin talk

As they cruise the oceans, dolphins stay in contact using a complex language of whistles, chirps, and clicks. Hunting dolphins use sound to locate their prey, emitting bursts of loud clicks and listening for the echoes. They even use sound to scare fish into a tight bait ball so they are easier to catch.

A dolphin can stun a fish with a powerful pulse of low-pitched sound.

High fliers

These flying fish use their extra-long fins as wings, bursting up out of the water and gliding through the air just above the waves for 160 ft (50 m) or more. They do this to escape from hunters lurking beneath the surface, but are often picked off by seabirds instead!

Weird and wonderful

Spinner dolphin

All oceanic dolphins are acrobats, but the spinner dolphin excels itself by leaping from the water and spinning in the air before falling back with a splash.

Amazon river dolphin

Found only in South America, the long-beaked, pink-skinned Amazon river dolphin is almost blind, and relies on echolocation to find prey such as fish and crabs.

Harbor porpoise

A porpoise is like a small dolphin, but has a rounded head with no beak. As its name implies, it is often seen in harbors and bays, preferring shallow waters.

Sleek swimmers

With their fishlike, streamlined bodies, dolphins are perfectly adapted for life at sea. Their ancestors were four-legged animals that lived on land, but they have lost their back limbs altogether. Instead they have broad tail flukes that are moved up and down by powerful muscles, driving them through the water and even through the air at up to 30 mph (50 kph).

Dolphins are so intelligent that they can use tools and even learn human sign language.

Kelp forest

The coastal fringes of cool seas to the north and south of the tropics are often carpeted with tough seaweeds known as kelp. In some places, such as the California coast, giant kelp can grow to incredible heights, forming dense underwater forests. These are rich in food for various types of fish and other animals such as sea otters and giant octopuses.

In the underwater forest

1 Pacific giant octopus
2 Wolf eel
3 Purple-ringed topshells
4 Blue rockfish
5 Sea otter

6 Pacific seahorse
7 Giant kelp
8 California sheephead fish
9 Kelp crab
10 Purple sea urchins

Ocean beanstalk

Fronds
Dotted along the kelp fronds are small gas-filled floats. These keep the top of each plant near the surface, where it gets the light it needs to grow.

Holdfasts
Kelp stems grow from rootlike holdfasts that are securely attached to rocks, providing an incredibly strong anchor for a plant that can grow up to 164 ft (50 m) or more.

Blue shoal
Shoals of blue rockfish swim among the tall kelp fronds, using their small mouths to take tiny planktonic animals from the water. The cool seas where the kelp forests grow are rich in plankton, unlike tropical oceans.

Powerful killer
Lurking among the kelp fronds is the world's biggest octopus—the Pacific giant octopus. Up to 5 ft (1.5 m) long, it catches crabs, clams, and even fish in its flexible suckered arms and then devours them with its tough, parrotlike beak.

Clam-crusher
A rock crevice on the seabed makes an ideal home for the wolf eel. This powerful fish is not as ferocious as it looks, but its immensely strong jaws can easily crush a crab or clam. It rarely leaves its hideout unless forced out by a bigger wolf eel.

Sea snails
Purple-ringed topshells creep over rocks and kelp fronds in search of their next meal. They feed mainly on microscopic algae, which they scrape off the surface with their filelike tongues.

Daring divers

Off Alaska and California, sea otters hunt for shellfish among the kelp forests. Their favorite prey are the spiny sea urchins that graze on the kelp. The otters dive to the bottom to catch the urchins, then carry them to the surface where they break them open so they can eat their soft flesh.

Clinging on

Delicate seahorses cling to the kelp fronds with their muscular tails to keep themselves from being swept away by ocean currents. They feed on tiny animals drifting in the water.

Crunch time

The crabs, lobsters, sea urchins, and other shellfish living near the floor of the kelp forest provide the California sheephead fish with plenty of prey. It crunches them up with its mouthful of extra-large teeth.

Pincer grip

Red kelp crabs browse on the young kelp, keeping a tight grip on the fronds to avoid being washed away. But they are often swept off their perches by winter storms, and fall victim to crab-eating predators, such as kelp fish and sea otters.

Nibbling urchins

Armies of purple sea urchins attack the kelp, shredding it with the tough toothlike structures in their mouths. If they were not eaten by sea otters, they would destroy much of the kelp forest.

Giant kelp can grow at the astonishing rate of 2 ft (60 cm) a day.

Top predator

Massively powerful, and armed with a set of teeth that can slice through its victims like a chainsaw, the great white shark is the most lethal fish in the sea. Apart from the killer whale it has no enemies, for no other hunter dares take it on. This makes it a top predator—the unchallenged end of the food chain. It is the biggest of the killer sharks, and the only one that regularly targets marine mammals such as seals. Acute senses lead it to its prey with deadly precision, and once in its sights they stand little chance of escape.

5

6

The jaws of a great white shark are powerful enough to chop a person in half.

7

9

8

Dedicated killer

1 Pilot fish
2 Great white shark
3 Massive gills
4 Sickle-shaped tail
5 Pointed snout
6 Supersensitive nostrils
7 Thrusting upper jaw
8 Saw-edged teeth
9 Bluefin tuna

Spectacular sharks

Hammerhead shark
A hammerhead shark's weird winglike head acts as a prey-finding scanner. It is peppered with special sensors that can detect faint electrical signals from prey, and the widely spaced eyes and nostrils are ideally placed to pinpoint a victim's exact location.

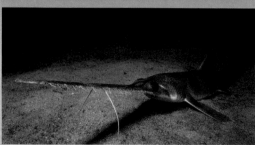

Sawshark
The upper jaw of a sawshark is extended into a long blade edged with sharp teeth. The shark uses it to attack prey on the seabed. As animals swim up in alarm it slashes with the saw to cripple them, making them easier to catch.

Thresher shark
Many sharks have big tail fins, but the thresher shark's tail is gigantic—almost as long as its body. The shark uses the scythe-shaped tail to herd and disable fish, sweeping it sideways through a shoal to stun as many as possible.

The earliest fossils of great white sharks are about 16 million years old.

Constant companions
These black-striped pilot fish seem to be taking a big risk by trailing the shark wherever it goes, hoping for a free meal of leftovers. But the shark leaves them alone because they do it a favor by removing bloodsucking parasites from its skin. It even lets the pilot fish swim into its mouth to pick food scraps from its teeth. Their stripes help the shark recognize them as its friends.

The great white shark has been ruthlessly tracked down and killed by shark hunters. It is so rare now that it is likely to become extinct.

Super senses

The shark can detect the slightest taint of blood in the water and track it from almost 1 mile (1.6 km) away. As it gets closer, pressure sensors on its head and flanks pick up vibrations from moving prey, and electrical detectors on its nose sense the tiny signals generated by its victim's nervous system. The combination allows the great white shark to home in on its target like a guided missile.

On the menu

The great white shark certainly attacks people, but most of its victims are bitten just once and not eaten. It seems that the shark doesn't like the way we taste! Its favorite prey are seals, dolphins, and small whales, but it will also snap up big fish like this tuna.

Killing machine

The shark's teeth are like triangular saw-edged razors, up to about 3 in (7 cm) long. As they get blunt they drop off and are replaced with new teeth moving up from behind, so the great white shark is always fully armed. As it charges into the attack its jaws gape open, with its mobile top jaw thrust forward. When the shark punches into its victim its jaws snap shut to chop out a great chunk of flesh. Even if the great white shark does nothing else, the effect is usually fatal.

The great white shark has plenty of spare teeth. It can go through about 20,000 teeth during its lifetime.

43

Ocean drifters

Drifting through the world's oceans like animated flowers, jellyfish live by snaring other animals in their stinging tentacles and then gathering them up to digest them. Most feed on the tiny creatures that swarm in the plankton, but some catch bigger prey such as fish and squid. A few, like the tropical box jellyfish, are among the most venomous creatures on Earth.

Stinging traps

1 Box jellyfish
2 Stinging tentacles
3 Sea nettle
4 Spotted jellyfish
5 Pacific butterfish

3

4

5

The box jellyfish kills more people each year than any other marine animal.

Ghostly drifters

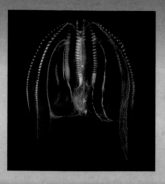

Comb jelly
Transparent comb jellies feed on the clouds of tiny creatures that drift in the ocean, reeling them in with their whiplike tentacles. To swim, they make rippling movements with rows of tiny hairs running down their bodies. When these catch the light, they create glittering patterns of color.

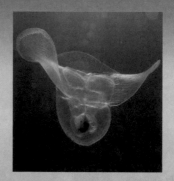

Sea butterfly
The sea butterflies are relatives of slugs and snails. They fly through the sea on winglike fins and eat tiny drifting animals, which they snare in nets of sticky slime. Like many sea creatures, they hide in deep dark water by day and rise to the surface at night to feed.

Deadly sting

It may look harmless, even beautiful, but the box jellyfish of the tropical Pacific is a killer. Hanging from each bottom corner of its box-shaped body is a bunch of 15 very long tentacles, each armed with thousands of stingers. The jellyfish uses them to catch prey, but if a person gets tangled up in the tentacles, the stings cause agonizing pain. They can even stop a person's heart—with deadly effect.

The lion's mane jellyfish is the longest animal on Earth, with tentacles 118 ft (36 m) long.

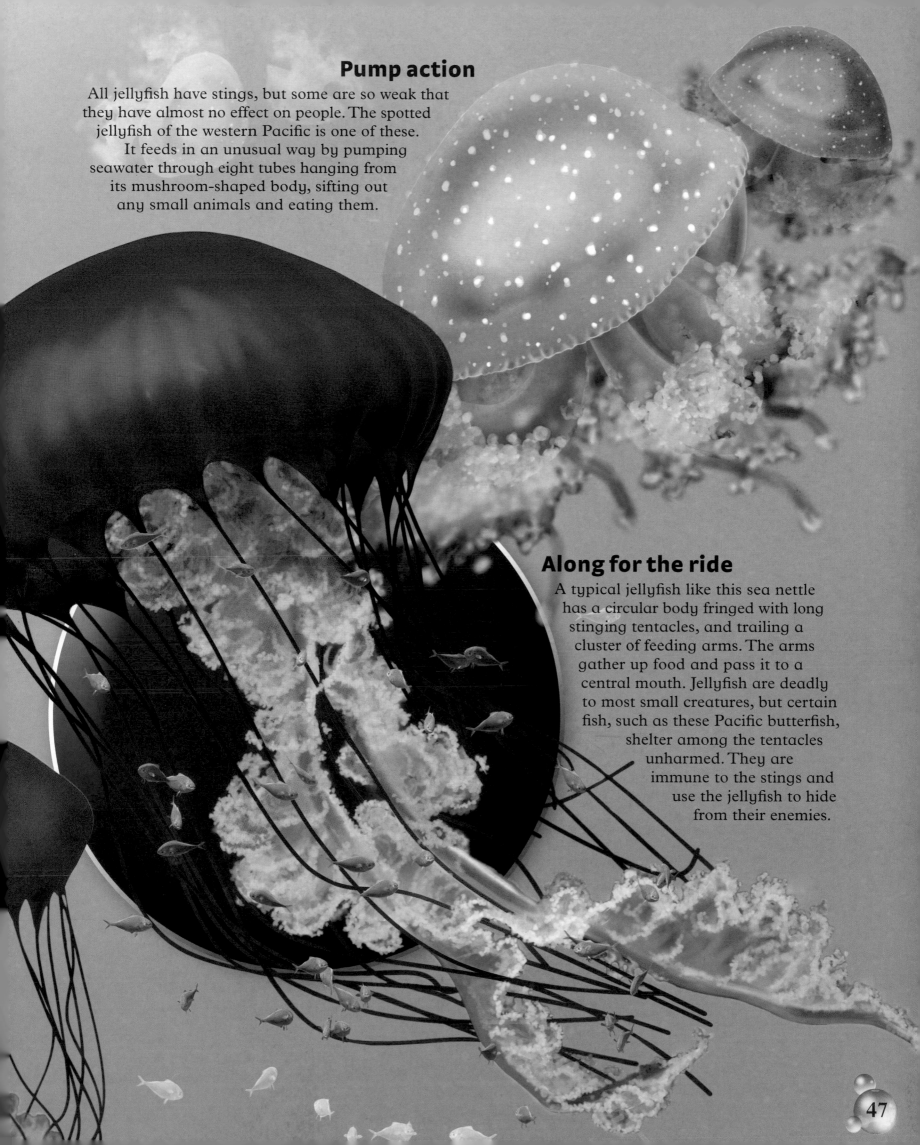

Pump action

All jellyfish have stings, but some are so weak that they have almost no effect on people. The spotted jellyfish of the western Pacific is one of these. It feeds in an unusual way by pumping seawater through eight tubes hanging from its mushroom-shaped body, sifting out any small animals and eating them.

Along for the ride

A typical jellyfish like this sea nettle has a circular body fringed with long stinging tentacles, and trailing a cluster of feeding arms. The arms gather up food and pass it to a central mouth. Jellyfish are deadly to most small creatures, but certain fish, such as these Pacific butterfish, shelter among the tentacles unharmed. They are immune to the stings and use the jellyfish to hide from their enemies.

9

A newborn baby sperm whale weighs as much as a small family car.

Titanic struggle

1 Sperm whale
2 Single blowhole
3 Wrinkled, scarred skin
4 Conical teeth
5 Giant squid
6 Muscular arms
7 Long, slender tentacles
8 Short flippers
9 Tail flukes

8

Battle zone

Just 1,000 ft (300 m) below the waves lies the dimly lit world of the twilight zone. This is the hunting ground of the sperm whale, an air-breathing giant that can hold its breath for an amazing 40 minutes as it dives in search of its main prey, deepwater squid. These include giant squid up to 46 ft (14 m) long, which fight back using toothed suckers that leave deep circular scars in the whale's skin.

1

2

3

The sperm whale has the largest brain of any animal on Earth.

4

5

7

6

Creatures of the deep

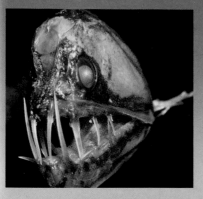

Viperfish
Like many of the predators that live in the ocean depths, this fearsome hunter has incredibly long teeth that close on its victims like a trap. Prey is so hard to find in the twilight zone—and in the dark zone below it—that any animal that manages to catch a meal must make absolutely sure it has no chance of escape.

Hairy angler fish
Deepwater anglers save energy by waiting for prey to swim into range. The hairy angler bristles with long sensory spines that detect any movement in the dark water, so it knows when a possible victim is near. When the time is right it opens its huge mouth so water rushes in, carrying its prey with it.

Gulper eel
Even weirder than the viperfish, the gulper eel is equipped with a huge mouth and a stomach that can stretch like a balloon. This allows it to engulf fish and other animals that are bigger than its own body. It has small eyes on the tip of its snout, and its monstrous jaws are lined with tiny, sharp teeth.

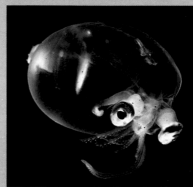

Glass squid
The body of a glass squid is dotted with special cells that produce light, so it glows in the dark. Many other creatures of the deep do this. Some use light to flash messages at each other, while others use it to find prey. A few generate a faint blue glow that matches the light filtering down from the surface, making them invisible.

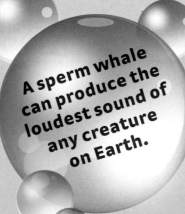

A sperm whale can produce the loudest sound of any creature on Earth.

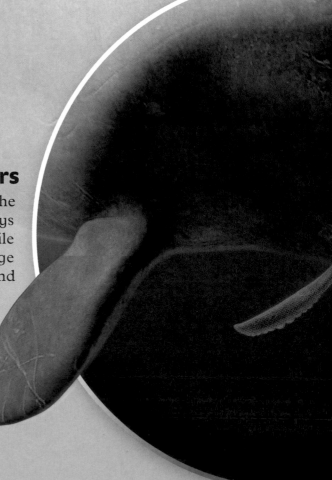

Deep divers
Even though it has to breathe air, the colossal sperm whale regularly stays underwater for well over half an hour while hunting. It can do this because it stores large amounts of vital oxygen in its blood and muscles. In fact, it breathes out before it dives, rather than breathing in. But when it comes back to the surface it has to breathe hard for about 10 minutes before it can dive again.

Huge head

The head of a sperm whale is gigantic, accounting for a third of the whale's length. A big male could have a head up to 23 ft (7 m) long, with a huge boxy snout that is filled with an oily fluid called spermaceti. The skin of this whale is pitted with long scratches and circular scars, inflicted by the sharp-toothed suckers of giant squid fighting for their lives in the ocean depths.

Spermaceti oil is used to oil the moving parts of spacecraft in the extreme cold of outer space.

About the size of a football, the eyes of a giant squid are bigger than those of any other animal on Earth.

Elusive squid

Very little is known about the mysterious giant squid. It lives deep in the twilight zone, and until recently no one had ever seen one alive. It preys on other squid and deep-sea fish, seizing them with a pair of extra-long feeding tentacles. Like other squid it is jet-propelled, blasting a jet of water out of its body cavity to shoot backward out of danger.

floor covered by layers of soft ooze—the remains of dead plankton that have drifted down through at least 10,000 ft (3,000 m) of dark water. This debris is sifted by creatures that spend their lives here, alongside scavengers that pick at the carcasses of fish and other dead animals.

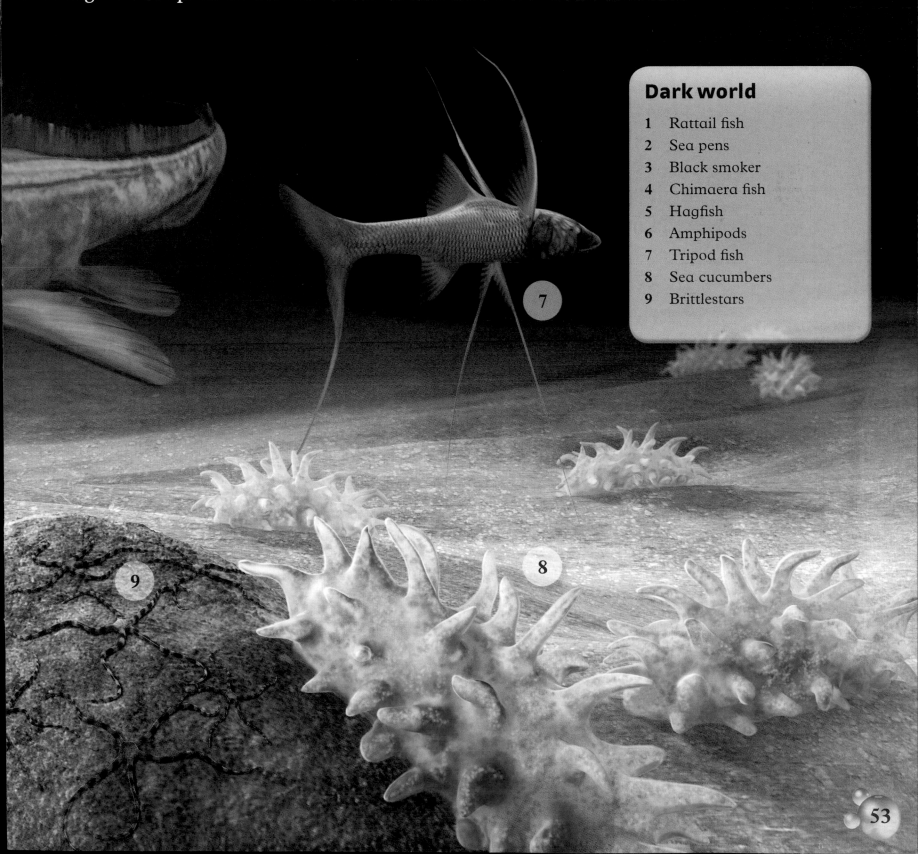

Dark world

1 Rattail fish
2 Sea pens
3 Black smoker
4 Chimaera fish
5 Hagfish
6 Amphipods
7 Tripod fish
8 Sea cucumbers
9 Brittlestars

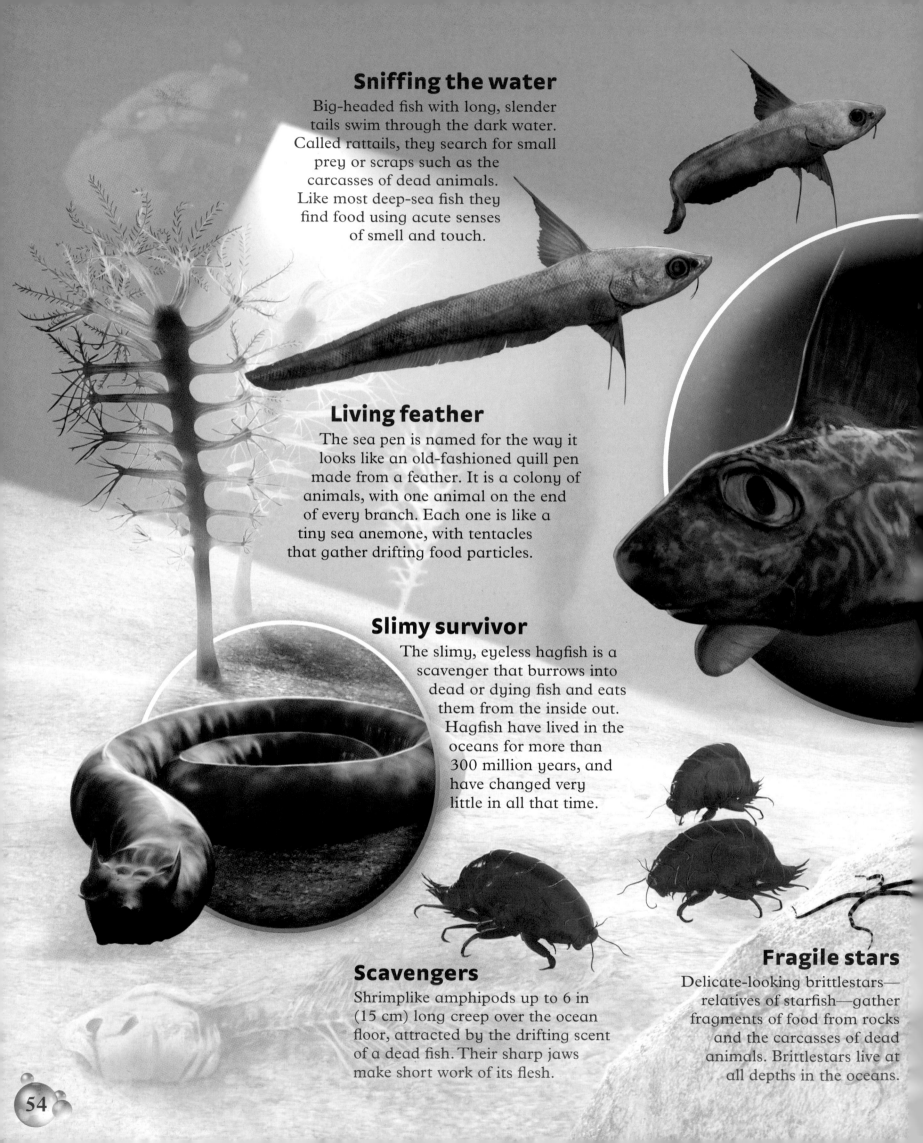

Sniffing the water

Big-headed fish with long, slender tails swim through the dark water. Called rattails, they search for small prey or scraps such as the carcasses of dead animals. Like most deep-sea fish they find food using acute senses of smell and touch.

Living feather

The sea pen is named for the way it looks like an old-fashioned quill pen made from a feather. It is a colony of animals, with one animal on the end of every branch. Each one is like a tiny sea anemone, with tentacles that gather drifting food particles.

Slimy survivor

The slimy, eyeless hagfish is a scavenger that burrows into dead or dying fish and eats them from the inside out. Hagfish have lived in the oceans for more than 300 million years, and have changed very little in all that time.

Scavengers

Shrimplike amphipods up to 6 in (15 cm) long creep over the ocean floor, attracted by the drifting scent of a dead fish. Their sharp jaws make short work of its flesh.

Fragile stars

Delicate-looking brittlestars— relatives of starfish—gather fragments of food from rocks and the carcasses of dead animals. Brittlestars live at all depths in the oceans.

Clam-cruncher

A slow-moving chimaera swims close to the soft ocean floor, searching for buried shellfish to crunch up in its tough jaws. These odd-looking fish are related to sharks and rays, and like them they have skeletons made of gristly cartilage.

Black smoker
In some parts of the ocean floor hot volcanic water pours from cracks in the rock. The water is black with chemicals that some microbes can use to generate energy and make food. This supports dense colonies of deep-ocean life.

Giant tubeworms
Huge marine worms live around the black smokers. Each has a colony of food-making microbes in its body.

Vent crabs
Blind white crabs scuttle over the ocean floor near the hot-water vents, feeding on the colonies of microbes.

Exploring the ocean floor is so difficult that scientists know more about the surface of the Moon.

High heels

The elegant tripod fish stands on the ocean floor, supported by three very long, stiff fin rays. Facing into the current, it uses its other fins to detect vibrations in the water that could be made by animals—allowing it to target and catch its prey.

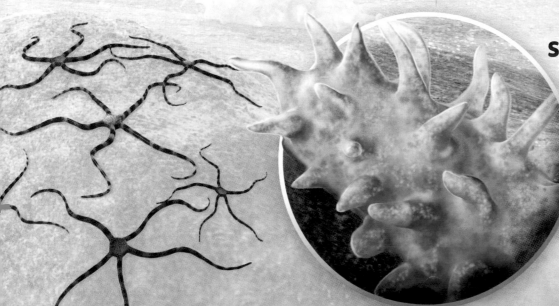

Sifting the ooze

Deepwater sea cucumbers glide over the ooze, scooping it up and swallowing it to digest anything edible. These relatives of starfish and sea urchins have sausagelike bodies, sometimes adorned with soft, fleshy spikes.

Glossary

Algae
Plantlike living things that can use the energy of sunlight to make food. Most oceanic algae are too small to see without a microscope, and drift in the water where they are eaten by small animals. Seaweeds are also algae, but are much bigger.

Blowhole
The nostrils of a whale or a dolphin, which are positioned on top of the head. The blowhole is used for breathing, and it can be closed when the animal dives.

Camouflage
Anything involving color, pattern, or shape that makes something such as an animal harder to see against its background.

Cartilage
Rubbery material that forms part of an animal's skeleton, but is not hard bone. The skeletons of sharks and rays are made of cartilage.

Colony
A group of animals or other living things that live together. A colony can be permanent or it can form briefly for a purpose, such as breeding in seabirds.

Dorsal
Refers to a feature on top of an animal's body, such as the triangular fin on the back of a shark.

Echolocation
Making sharp sounds and listening for the echoes that reflect off nearby objects. Producing and receiving a continuous stream of sound builds up an image from the echoes.

Filter-feeding
Using a sievelike system to strain food from the water. Most oceanic filter-feeders strain the water through their gills.

Flippers
Finlike structures that are basically flattened wings, arms, or legs.

Flukes
Extensions of a whale's or a dolphin's tail that look like a fish's tail fin.

Food chain
A food pathway that connects several different species. Food passes from plants to animals, and then from one animal to another as predators feed on their prey.

Fronds
The leaflike parts of seaweeds such as kelp. They are not true leaves, because they do not have the same internal structure.

Holdfast
The rootlike part of a seaweed that anchors its stem and keeps it from floating away.

Iceberg
A big chunk of floating ice that has broken off the end of a coastal glacier or ice shelf.

Krill
Small shrimplike animals that live in open oceans. They live all over the world, but are most numerous in the Southern Ocean, where they form a vital food source for many Antarctic animals.

Mammal
A warm-blooded animal that feeds its young on milk. Marine mammals include seals, sea lions, sea otters, whales, and dolphins.

Microbe
A tiny, simple organism that can be seen only with a microscope. Includes organisms such as bacteria.

Microscopic
Describes anything that is too small to see without the aid of a microscope.

Pack ice
Pieces of ice of different sizes and ages that have been driven together to form an almost continuous sheet.

Parasite
Any living thing that lives in or on another living thing and steals something from it. A leech that sucks the blood of an animal is a parasite.

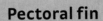

Pectoral fin
The pair of fins just behind a fish's head. They are used for steering and sometimes for propulsion.

Plankton
Living things that drift in the water near the sunlit surface. Most are very small, including tiny floating algae that make food, and small animals that eat the algae.

Pod
An extended family group of whales or dolphins.

Predator
An animal that catches other live animals, kills them, and eats them.

Prey
Any animal that is killed and eaten by another animal (a predator).

Scales
Small, tough plates that grow from the skin of an animal such as a fish, and protect it from damage and disease.

Scavenger
An animal that feeds on the remains of dead animals, either as a regular habit or occasionally.

Streamlined
Having a smooth shape that glides through the water (or air) easily.

Venomous
Describes any animal that is armed with venom—a poison that is deliberately injected into its enemies by a sting or specialized fangs.

Sea ice
Ice that forms on the ocean surface as seawater freezes. There are many types, including pack ice.

Submersible
A specialized type of submarine that can dive very deeply, and is used mainly for scientific research.

Vent
A hole that something flows through. In the oceans, water heated by hot volcanic rock beneath the ocean floor erupts through hydrothermal vents, often known as black smokers.

Shellfish
Oceanic animals with shells of some sort.

Swarm
A large group of small animals—so big that there are far too many of them to count.

Stranded
Describes an oceanic animal that has accidentally become stuck on a beach. When this happens to whales, they usually die.

Tropics
The warm regions of the world near the equator, lying between the Tropic of Cancer and the Tropic of Capricorn.

Index

Acknowledgments

Dorling Kindersley would like to thank Carron Brown for the index and proofreading, John Searcy for Americanization, and Ben Morgan for editorial assistance.

The publisher would like to thank the following for their kind permission to reproduce their photographs:

(Key: a-above; b-below/bottom; c-center; f-far; l-left; r-right; t-top)

6-7 Corbis: Kazuya Tanaka/amanaimages (background). **Science Photo Library:** Tom Van Sant, Geosphere Project/Planetary Visions (c). **10 Corbis:** Alaska Stock (bl). **Getty Images:** Frank Krahmer/Photographer's Choice RF (clb). **11 Corbis:** Alissa Crandall (tc); Hans Strand (tl). **15 Getty Images:** Oxford Scientific/Gerard Soury (tc); Oxford Scientific/David B. Fleetham (c). **18 Corbis:** Andy Murch/Visuals Unlimited (cla). **SuperStock:** Age Fotostock (tl). **22 Alamy Images:** Chris Gomersall (tl). **23 Getty Images:** Iconica/Frans Lemmens (c). **26 Corbis:** Jeffrey L. Rotman (tr); Denis Scott (tl); Anna C.J. Segeren/Specialist Stock (tc). **30 Corbis:** Amos Nachoum (bl); Lawson Wood (cla); Norbert Wu/Science Faction (cl). **SeaPics. com:** Masa Ushioda (clb). **35 Alamy Images:** Andrea Innocenti/CuboImages srl (tc). **Corbis:** Anthony Pierce/Specialist Stock (tl); Kevin Schafer (tr). **38 Corbis:** Richard Herrmann/Visuals Unlimited (fcla). **Getty Images:** Oxford Scientific/Tobias Bernhard (ftl). **42 Alamy Images:** Marty Snyderman/Stephen Frink Collection (cla); WaterFrame (cl). **Corbis:** Amos Nachoum (tl). **46 Corbis:** Frans Lanting (tl); David Wrobel/Visuals Unlimited (tr). **50 DeepSeaPhotography.com:** Peter Batson (cra). **imagequestmarine.com:** (tr). **Science Photo Library:** Gregory Ochocki (tl). **SuperStock:** Minden Pictures (cla). **55 Corbis:** Ralph White (tl, tr). **DeepSeaPhotography. Com:** Peter Batson (cra).

All other images © Dorling Kindersley
For further information see:
www.dkimages.com